To

_____

From

_____

Date

_____

As Grandpa Says

Nick Harrison

ARTWORK BY

Audrey Jeanne Roberts

HARVEST HOUSE PUBLISHERS

EUGENE, OREGON

As Grandpa Says

Text copyright © 2012 by Nick Harrison
Artwork copyright © 2012 by Audrey Jeanne Roberts. Courtesy of MHS Licensing.

Published by Harvest House Publishers
Eugene, Oregon 97402
www.harvesthousepublishers.com

ISBN 978-0-7369-3849-5

MHS Licensing
11100 Wayzata Blvd., Suite 550
Minneapolis, MN 55305
www.mhslicensing.com

Design and production by Garborg Design Works, Savage, Minnesota

To learn more about the author and his books, go to www.nickharrisonbooks.com

Printed in China

12 13 14 15 16 17 18 19 / FC / 10 9 8 7 6 5 4 3 2 1

FOR

Joshua, Emma,
Matthew, and Abbi

GRANDPA'S WISDOM

Each New Day Is a Gift, and That's Why They Call It the *Present*

God gave us memories that we might have roses in December.

—J.M. Barrie

I love growing older. When I was young, I didn't think much about aging. Back then it was all about...well, being young. And that was fine. I created a lot of good memories doing those youthful things like making a cross-country road trip and living in a commune. I'll never forget the time I took my date to a formal dance on a Saturday night in San Francisco. Afterward we walked in our formal wear through Haight-Ashbury, expecting to garner odd looks from all the jeans-wearing, tie-dyed-T-shirt-clad, sandal-trod hippies. We were surprised to find out that in some weird way we fit right in. They didn't give us a second look.

Through the years, I've come to realize that as long as I'm alive, there will be more memories to add to my collection. That's true of all of us. We each are given a mental memory album in which we can continue pasting new entries. We will never grow too old to add more. Each day is indeed a gift—a chance to grow in God, to love life, and to add more pages to the album.

Never stop collecting memories. *Never.*

Men shall speak of the might
of Your awesome acts,
and I will declare
Your greatness.
They shall utter the memory
of Your great goodness,
and shall sing of Your
righteousness.

Psalm 145:6-7

Give God Room

But God—see God act! He changes all by His touch! This "But God" is the bridge that leads us out of our dark and hopeless condition. When all human strength is at an end—"But God."

—Henrietta Mears

Almost daily we hear of friends facing deep waters—illnesses, money, family, or church woes—the stuff of which life is made.

I have a theory, though. God didn't design life to be the proverbial bowl of cherries. If not through deep waters, then how can God show Himself strong on our behalf? That's surely what He wants to do, but often we don't give God room to work. We're like the overeager father who baits his son's hook rather than lets the boy learn to do it himself. We rush in and try to fix situations that are really unfixable unless God steps in. I think sometimes God watches and waits until we've exhausted our own resources and cry out, "Help me, God!"

That's when we finally give God room to work. And that's when miracles happen.

BUT GOD...

Ephesians 2:4

Garbage in, Garbage Out

*If you will not determine to be pure,
you will grow more and more impure.*

—George MacDonald

No longer do we live in a *Leave It to Beaver* world. Frankly, I wonder if we ever really did. As a grandpa watching the little ones come along behind me, I worry about what their eyes see and what their ears hear—particularly on TV, at the movies, and even in books. I worry that while I once wanted to be like Wally Cleaver, some young kids may want to be like Bart Simpson or one of those creepy South Park kids.

I read somewhere that during the growing-up years, each day a typical child watches four hours of TV plus puts in an additional two hours on a computer or playing video games. I don't think it's possible to watch that much TV and not be exposed to far too much violence, bad language, and sexual immorality. I believe that what goes into a child's mind will eventually come out in their actions.

"Garbage in, garbage out" is Grandpa's new way of stating the old saw, "As the twig is bent, so grows the tree."

I think it's written somewhere in our job specs as grandpas that we can influence our grandkids in the right direction. Something like: "Grandpa's wisdom in, Grandpa's wisdom out." I like that.

Lord, save us from a generation of crooked trees. Help dads and moms and grandpas and grandmas grow those little saplings straight and strong, and if they must bend, let them bend toward the light, not the dark.

I WILL SET NOTHING
WICKED BEFORE MY EYES.

Psalm 101:3

A Cord of Three Strands Is Not Easily Broken

Rise up, O men of God!
Have done with lesser things.
Give heart and mind and soul and strength
to serve the King of kings.

—William P. Merrill

When I was a boy, a bunch of us kids gathered on the playground to play games like red rover. We would yell, "Red rover, red rover, send Billy right over!" Billy would then race across the distance from his team to our team and try to break through our line as we stood with interlocked arms. We stood strong, daring him to break our grasp and score for his team. There's great power in linking arms against impending danger.

Now that I'm a man, I still "link arms," but here's the difference. I link up with a few men who are part of my "cord of three strands." Like the Bible's David and Jonathan and Jesus and His disciple John, we spiritually link arms and support one another when problems happen. They pray for me, counsel me when necessary, and cheer me on in my latest ventures. I'm blessed to have these men in my life.

Although men sometimes prefer friendships of a more casual nature, hardly the kind of relationship where a man can bear his soul without fear of somebody—his friends or himself—becoming embarrassed, my friends and I are creating our own story of friendships, one struggle and one victory at a time.

Good men, all.

If the "Billys" in your life are breaking through weak arms, dare to find some good men with whom you can link arms.

THOUGH ONE MAY BE OVERPOWERED BY ANOTHER,
TWO CAN WITHSTAND HIM.
AND A THREEFOLD CORD IS NOT QUICKLY BROKEN.

Ecclesiastes 4:12

If a Job Is Worth Doing, It Is Worth Doing Well

I would prefer even to fail with honor than to win by cheating.

—Sophocles

It's funny, the things we remember. When I was a freshman in high school, Mrs. Little was my English teacher. She was a good teacher, and I was an average student, which meant that I wasn't beneath taking a shortcut when it came to doing my homework. One of Mrs. Little's assignments was a book report. Procrastinator that I was, I put off finding a book to read until the last minute. Then I had a brilliant idea: Why not watch a movie that was based on a book and write my report from that?

I checked the TV listings. Sure enough, that very night I could watch "Drums Along the Mohawk," starring Henry Fonda and Claudette Colbert. It was based on a book by Walter D. Edmonds. So I watched the movie, and it was terrific. I immediately went to my bedroom desk and wrote a glowing book report. In fact it glowed so much that

Mrs. Little recommended a few more books I might enjoy, gave me a very good grade, and patted me on the back.

Somehow getting that good grade didn't feel quite as good as I thought it would. Neither did the good grade Mr. Padilla gave me in my high school Spanish class after I read the English translation of a book we were assigned to read in Spanish.

Doing a job well means doing it *right*. No cutting corners. No cheating. I suppose the fact that I remember those assignments all these decades later (and have forgotten every other assignment I was given) is a good sign that I learned my lesson. Now when offered a job to do, I weigh the question. Can I do this job effectively? And if so, I put myself into it. I do a job that would make Mrs. Little proud of me for the right reasons.

What was *your* high school shortcut? I bet you remember it well and for the same reason I remember. Let's agree to no more shortcuts when we're asked to do a job. Let's do it right.

WHATEVER YOU DO, DO IT HEARTILY, AS TO THE LORD AND NOT TO MEN.

Colossians 3:23

A Journey of a Thousand Miles

He who is outside his door has the hardest part of his journey behind him.

—Dutch Proverb

Grandma and I like to travel by train. We enjoy watching the view roll by without the distractions that driving requires. If the view isn't so desirable, we can read a book or spend a few minutes checking our eyelids for holes (if you get my drift).

Every time we go on a lengthy trip by train, I wonder anew at the work that went into laying the transcontinental track. It's the kind of momentous task that, had I been in charge, I would have taken one look at the project on paper and turned in my resignation. Thank God the person who made that decision had the vision for the entire job—not just the first few miles—and followed through. Of course, credit must go to the tireless workers who shed much sweat during the backbreaking work as they accomplished such a feat one mile at a time.

Though the larger tasks I've been given in life pale in comparison with that of laying the rail, they all share one simple truth: Taking the first few steps—as small as they may be—brings me that much closer to the distant completion of the task. Regarding larger tasks, we must often wait until the project is entirely finished to experience the greatest sense of fulfillment. That's why 150 years after it was completed, I'm still marveling at the task those rail layers accomplished.

I think we make a mistake when we shrink from larger projects. We reason that we can't finish such a big job, that it will bring too much pain to complete, or we forget that beginning such a task is the hardest part. The closer we advance toward the goal, the brighter the vision for what we will have accomplished. We just need to slowly take that next step… and then the next one and the one after that. One. Step. At. A. Time.

LITTLE BY LITTLE I WILL DRIVE THEM OUT FROM BEFORE YOU, UNTIL YOU HAVE INCREASED, AND YOU INHERIT THE LAND.

Exodus 23:30

Remember the Lord!

We regard God as an airman regards his parachute; it's there for emergencies but he hopes he'll never have to use it.

—C.S. Lewis

Each morning as our kids headed off to school, I'd remind them to remember the Lord throughout their day. I was trying to instill in them the presence of mind that's backed by a thorough knowledge that God is involved in *all* our daily activities. Math final? God is there. Boring history lecture? God is there. Lunch with friends? God is there too.

He's in the classroom, the lunchroom, and even on the playground. Because He's always mindful of us, can we not also be mindful of Him throughout the day, no matter our activity?

When I was saying those words to the kids, I was also reminding myself to acknowledge that the Lord is there with me in my office at work. He's there during the business lunch. He's in the car with me during that bumper-to-bumper rush-hour traffic. He's even there with me while I'm working out at the gym.

As we age, daily remember the Lord. In the hospital for tests? He's there. In the loneliness of an empty nest? Sitting on a bench in the park? He's there. At the graveside of a recently departed loved one? Yes, He's there too.

Remembering that God is with us throughout the day gives us courage to know that nothing escapes His notice. We're always on His mind...even when He's not on ours.

In that, I have great reason to rejoice. We all do.

ARE NOT TWO SPARROWS SOLD FOR A COPPER COIN? AND NOT ONE OF THEM FALLS TO THE GROUND APART FROM YOUR FATHER'S WILL. BUT THE VERY HAIRS OF YOUR HEAD ARE ALL NUMBERED. DO NOT FEAR THEREFORE; YOU ARE OF MORE VALUE THAN MANY SPARROWS.

Matthew 10:29-31

One and God
Make a Majority

Right is right, even if everyone
is against it, and wrong is
wrong, even if everyone is for it.

—William Penn

I enjoy the old movies on TV or DVD more than the current theater offerings. They're lots cheaper too. The other night I watched Henry Fonda in *Twelve Angry Men*. The twelve men were on a jury, and the case seemed like a slam-dunk guilty verdict. But when the first vote was taken, the tally was eleven guilty and one not guilty (Fonda's character, of course). As can be imagined, the eleven men were not happy. So the rest of the movie is about Henry Fonda's character standing firm for his vote against the angry onslaught of the other jurors. By the movie's end, the vote is twelve not guilty to zero guilty.

What I like about the movie is the portrayal of one man's willingness to stick to his guns when he believes he's right. To endure the name-calling, the outburst of criticism, well, it takes someone special to do that.

In the Bible, Daniel was such a man. Early in the book bearing his name, Daniel refuses to alter his diet to accommodate the king's orders. Later Daniel is found worshipping the true God, violating an ordinance that no one was to worship any god or man except King Darius. He is thrust into the lions' den, but the next morning he remains untouched by the beasts. We read in Daniel 6:21-23:

Then Daniel said to the king, "O king, live forever! My God sent His angel and shut the lions' mouths, so that they have not hurt me, because I was found innocent before Him; and also, O king, I have done no wrong before you."

Now the king was exceedingly glad for him, and commanded that they should take Daniel up out of the den. So Daniel was taken up out of the den, and no injury whatever was found on him, because he believed in his God.

God stands with those who stand with Him. No compromise. I sure need Him standing by me. I know you do too.

AND IF IT SEEMS EVIL TO YOU TO SERVE THE LORD, CHOOSE FOR YOURSELVES THIS DAY WHOM YOU WILL SERVE, WHETHER THE GODS WHICH YOUR FATHERS SERVED THAT WERE ON THE OTHER SIDE OF THE RIVER, OR THE GODS OF THE AMORITES, IN WHOSE LAND YOU DWELL. BUT AS FOR ME AND MY HOUSE, WE WILL SERVE THE LORD.

Joshua 24:15

It's All in a Day's Work

The miracle is not that we do this work, but that we are happy to do it.

—Mother Teresa

Blessed is the grandpa who loves his work. That would be me. I thoroughly enjoy my job. Though I'm getting up in years, I'm happy to say that, for most of my adult life, I've had jobs that actually bordered on being fun. When I was in my twenties, I drove a bookmobile for the county library system for a few years. I remember thinking at the time, *I'd do this for free*! Of course, I never told my boss that.

Later jobs were almost as enjoyable—with just a couple of minor and short-lived exceptions—and for the most part, I think our work is meant to be that way. Work is meant to bring meaning to our life. What we do should in some way make a difference. No matter what the job, it can be a source of joy for us. Even the Seven Dwarfs could trudge off to their mines each day with a song.

But the place where we earn our salary isn't our only job assignment in this life. I remember the night our first child entered the world and I accepted the calling—and job—of being a father. Two more soon followed, and ever since then, I've accepted and loved the role God's given me as a father. As the kids grew, my role changed. Now that they're fully grown and on their own, I'm *still* their father, but I have different responsibilities. Then a few years ago, I accepted the new job of being a grandfather. What a glorious calling that is!

Thank God for all the jobs He gives us—especially the roles of father and grandfather, which earn us the least in dollars but actually produce the richest payment of all.

WHATEVER YOUR
HAND FINDS TO
DO, DO IT WITH
YOUR MIGHT.

Ecclesiastes 9:10

Leave It Better Than You Found It

What is common to many is taken least care of, for all men have greater regard for what is their own than for what they possess in common with others.

—Aristotle

Our church organizes an annual family camp each summer. We've been doing this for 36 years now, and we look forward to it all year long. We have some great times together. We eat, pray, play, and swim in the old swimming hole together, and when it's time to go home, we work together to leave the camp better than we found it.

Leaving something better than you found it is a principle that goes back many, many years. No doubt fathers have handed it down to their sons and mothers to their daughters through the generations. For example, my dad taught me to return a borrowed tool in better condition than I received it.

What would this old earth be like if every man and woman took action to make their part of the world better than when they first found it? Could all that energy we spend on fighting wars be better spent helping those who desperately need food? We have lots of challenges before us, but each one gives us the opportunity to thank God for life and change this planet for the better, especially in the things that matter most—loving God, ensuring freedom, honoring plain old morality, and making personal integrity a priority.

Though I can't do anyone else's share of bettering planet Earth, I'm sure going to do my share and hope others feel the same way. It's the right thing to do.

THEN GOD SAID, "LET US MAKE MAN IN OUR IMAGE, ACCORDING TO OUR LIKENESS; LET THEM HAVE DOMINION OVER THE FISH OF THE SEA, OVER THE BIRDS OF THE AIR, AND OVER THE CATTLE, OVER ALL THE EARTH AND OVER EVERY CREEPING THING THAT CREEPS ON THE EARTH." SO GOD CREATED MAN IN HIS OWN IMAGE; IN THE IMAGE OF GOD HE CREATED HIM; MALE AND FEMALE HE CREATED THEM. THEN GOD BLESSED THEM, AND GOD SAID TO THEM, "BE FRUITFUL AND MULTIPLY; FILL THE EARTH AND SUBDUE IT; HAVE DOMINION OVER THE FISH OF THE SEA, OVER THE BIRDS OF THE AIR, AND OVER EVERY LIVING THING THAT MOVES ON THE EARTH."

Genesis 1:26-28

If That Doesn't Light Your Fire, Your Wood's Too Wet

All thoughts, all passions, all delights,
Whatever stirs this mortal frame,
All are but ministers of Love,
And feed his sacred flame.

—Samuel Taylor Coleridge

Everyone ages. Some even grow old. When I realized I was getting along in years, I determined *not* to become a curmudgeon. We have plenty of fussbudgets already. I want to stay upbeat and excited about the life God's given me. I see each new day as an adventure waiting to happen.

As I unwrap my daily adventure, I can't much abide it when some sour old grump pours water on my wood by telling me what's wrong with it, why it's not an adventure at all, or that I'm too old for adventures. The truth is

I pity the man. He's not really living; he's just biding time until he can slip into his grave. That's not me! Although I have yet to take my first bungee jump or reserve my spot on the skydiving team, the blood in these old veins is still percolating pretty hot.

I told Grandma the other day that I was thinking about taking up the skateboard. When I was a boy, we made skateboards by nailing our old metal skates to a sawed-off two-by-four. They are so much fancier nowadays! When I asked Grandma about where I might find a big parking lot to practice skateboarding, she gave me "the look" and suggested the hospital parking lot. But even that didn't dampen my wood. Come this Christmas, I'm asking Santa for my first skateboard. I just hope Grandma doesn't have a word with him first.

I think God wants us all—young and old—to keep our wood dry because when He sets a match to it, the fun begins. Woe to the man whose wood won't catch because he's been pouring the water of discontent over it.

Grandpa, if your wood's a tad damp, let the sun shine hard on it and dry it out. You've got some adventures waiting. See you in the hospital parking lot!

I WAS MUTE WITH SILENCE,
I HELD MY PEACE EVEN FROM GOOD;
AND MY SORROW WAS STIRRED UP.
MY HEART WAS HOT WITHIN ME;
WHILE I WAS MUSING, THE FIRE BURNED.
THEN I SPOKE WITH MY TONGUE:
"LORD, MAKE ME TO KNOW MY END,
AND WHAT IS THE MEASURE OF MY DAYS,
THAT I MAY KNOW HOW FRAIL I AM."

Psalm 39:2-4

Measure Twice and Cut Once

*Never be in a hurry;
do everything quietly
and in a calm spirit.
Do not lose your inner
peace for anything
whatsoever, even if
your whole world
seems upset.*

—Saint Francis de Sales

Grandma tells me that she's always careful when she measures and cuts fabric for her quilts, but if she makes a minor mistake, the fabric can stretch just a tad, and she can make do. In the woodshop, that's not the case. I wonder how many forests could have been saved if before applying the saw to the wood, the carpenter measured twice to make sure of his cut.

Even the best carpenter can make a mistake. That's why most good woodworkers make sure their measurements are correct before they cut. With my all-thumbs ability in the workshop, measuring four times would be necessary. Even then all bets are off on my accuracy.

I imagine even Noah made sure of his cuts before he applied the saw. God gave him the exact dimensions of the ark he was to build. Noah obeyed, and the rest is history.

God gives everyone the directions necessary to make the right cuts in life. If we make sure we've got it right before we make those cuts, we can have a happy, well-joined life. Life—like wood and unlike fabric—is hard to stretch when the measurements are wrong.

Brother, make sure of that cut before the saw touches the wood.

MY EYES SHALL BE ON THE FAITHFUL OF THE LAND,
THAT THEY MAY DWELL WITH ME;
HE WHO WALKS IN A PERFECT WAY,
HE SHALL SERVE ME.

Psalm 101:6

When an Old Man Dies, a Library Burns Down

If you wish for good advice, consult an old man.

—Romanian Proverb

My grandkids think of me as an old man. I don't mind it, really. When I was their age, I thought a thirty-year-old was over-the-hill. But when I turned thirty myself, I started to realize a few things about getting older. One thing is that we're never too old to keep learning lessons from the circumstances put before us—some lessons are easy; others are harder.

I think that every older person has a book or two in them. They could have a book of wisdom, sage advice, caution, exhortation, certainly humor, and even a few "go for its." The thing is, once a man or woman learns these things, God moves them on to heaven. That's not bad, mind you. In fact, it's the ultimate good. Still a man can't help but think how all he's learned might benefit the person just beginning their journey through life.

My own dad, great-grandpa to the grandkids, left this earth a few years ago. Although I miss his presence, I also miss his wisdom. I well remember the mistakes of my youth that could have been avoided if I'd shaken off my pride and listened to what he'd learned the hard way.

I suppose every generation is like that. Everyone has to learn their own way. The secret is to pass the test the first time we encounter the situation. Otherwise our life becomes a bit like the movie *Groundhog Day*. We have to take the same test again and then again, until we pass it. Smart folks learn fast, and even smarter ones listen to old men.

My son, hear the instruction of your father,
And do not forsake the law of your mother;
For they will be a graceful ornament on your head,
And chains about your neck.

Proverbs 1:8-9

You Can't Keep a Good Man Down

It's not whether you get knocked down; it's whether you get up.

—Vince Lombardi

When I think back at all the mistakes I've made, it makes me want a do-over… well, perhaps not on all my life, but on a few certain things. Marrying Grandma is one thing I'd do again in a heartbeat. But there was that time I betrayed a good friend without meaning to and the time I failed to speak up when something needed to be said. I remember many occasions when I should have remained silent…and didn't. What about that business failure or that long-standing grudge I had against…? Oh, well, why go on?

The fact is we've all made mistakes—plenty of them. But for me, I've experienced redemption by learning the lesson and moving on. Perhaps I didn't learn as quickly as I should have, but *eventually* I came to realize that football legend Vince Lombardi was right when he said, "It's not whether you get knocked down; it's whether you get up."

So I got up. Time and again, I rose slowly from my fall to find myself on my knees—a good place to be, by the way. From there I pulled myself up to full stature, released a deep breath, dusted myself off, and figured out what that exhausting

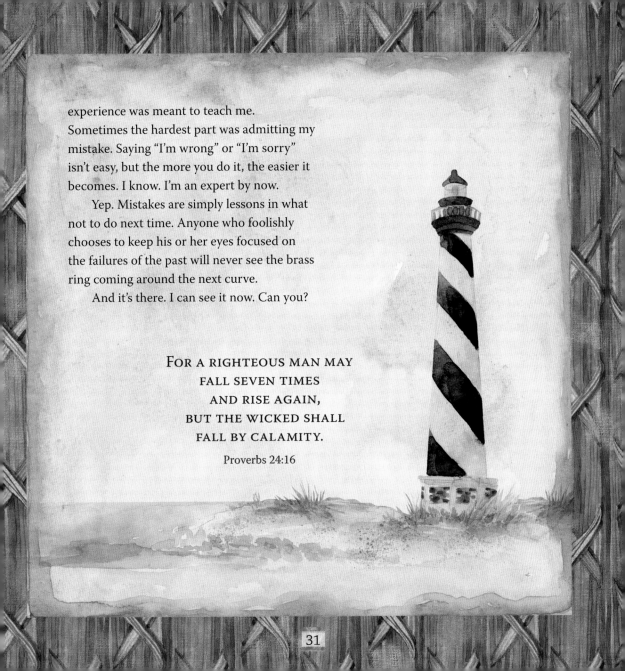

experience was meant to teach me.
Sometimes the hardest part was admitting my
mistake. Saying "I'm wrong" or "I'm sorry"
isn't easy, but the more you do it, the easier it
becomes. I know. I'm an expert by now.

Yep. Mistakes are simply lessons in what
not to do next time. Anyone who foolishly
chooses to keep his or her eyes focused on
the failures of the past will never see the brass
ring coming around the next curve.

And it's there. I can see it now. Can you?

FOR A RIGHTEOUS MAN MAY
FALL SEVEN TIMES
AND RISE AGAIN,
BUT THE WICKED SHALL
FALL BY CALAMITY.

Proverbs 24:16

The Only Way to Have a Friend Is to Be One

The better part of one's life consists of his friendships.

—Abraham Lincoln

Like many men, I have an ample supply of acquaintances but not nearly as many friends as I'd like. That's to be expected because a relationship with a friend goes deeper than one with a mere acquaintance. Friendships are made of iron and velvet and are built to wear. They're rare.

The very best friend I ever had—or ever will have—was Steve, a guy I met when we were sophomores in high school. Steve had this little yellow and white car—a Metropolitan. You don't see them around much anymore. On a dull weekend night, Steve and I would take that little Metro out to the hills, drive around, and talk about the deep issues of life. What kind of men would we be? What would we do with our lives? We talked about those sorts of things—topics you don't talk about with just anyone.

After high school, Steve and I became roommates at college. We even went out on some double dates together. In fact Steve agreed to be my best man when I married the girl he had dated before me. Then in his mid-thirties, Steve was diagnosed with cancer. He fought a good fight, but he died at 37. Far too young.

No, I'll never have a good friend like Steve again, but after Steve died, God did send along Mike, Ron, Dell, another Mike, and now another good friend named Steve. They are good men, every one of them. They are gifts to me from God—just as Steve was.

The secret to friendships this grandpa has found comes from the book of Proverbs in the Bible. King Solomon wrote, "A man who has friends must himself be friendly" (Proverbs 18:24). God will send friends our way. When they come, we have to recognize them as gifts and show ourselves friendly. You might think of it as sowing friendship seeds. Yes, sir, sow the friendship seed and in due season reap the friends.

I'm still planting those seeds in my life, and thank God, they're still sprouting a good crop.

A FRIEND LOVES AT ALL TIMES.

Proverbs 17:17

Wear the old coat and buy the new book

No man can be called friendless who has God and the companionship of good books.

—Elizabeth Barrett Browning

In an effort to keep up with technology, I've joined a couple of online forums. My user name is, to no one's surprise who knows me, "Bookman." Before I was Bookman, I suppose you could say I was "Bookboy." I've always loved books. I love to read them, collect them; just holding them in my hands fills me with wonder. While just a teen, my first job was shelving books in the local library. To this day, I'd say my favorite smell is that of an old library or used bookstore, chock-full of wisdom, humor, and plain good stories for anyone who'll sit down and quiet themselves long enough to savor a book.

When it comes to reading on those electronic gadgets, I'm a holdout. I have nothing against them personally. True, it's better to read on a Kindle or a Nook than not read at all, but for me, experiencing a book is more than the sum of the words inside. It's holding the book, touching the paper, even earmarking the last page you read.

The truth is that books take me somewhere else. Sometimes I venture into the crime world of New York City in the 1930s with detective Philo Vance as written by

S.S. Van Dine. I like to read novels about the westward migration of the nineteenth century in books like *My Ántonia* by Willa Cather or *The Emigrants* by Johan Bojer. I've been with Corrie Ten Boom in a Nazi prison and on the rough streets of the drug-infested hoods with David Wilkerson in *The Cross and the Switchblade*. I was even there with Brother Andrew smuggling Bibles into places where it was illegal.

One of the best gifts you can give your grandchildren is a love of reading. I'm starting mine now while they are young with Mother Goose stories, Aesop's fables, *Goodnight Moon* by Margaret Wise Brown, and *Pat the Bunny* by Dorothy Kunhardt. Eventually, we'll get to the Hardy Boys, Nancy Drew, Laura Ingalls Wilder, and to the Chronicles of Narnia and beyond.

It won't bother me a bit if the grandkids roll their eyes as they open yet another book present from Grandpa Bookman because I know they'll love what they find in those pages. One of these years, instead of a book, I'm going to get them their very own fancy bookcase—glass doors and all.

Do you remember your favorite childhood book? Have you given copies to your grandchildren yet? When you do, be sure to inscribe it with a warm note from Grandpa. In the years to come, they'll treasure that book and maybe eventually pass it on to their grandkids.

> BRING THE CLOAK THAT I LEFT WITH CARPUS AT TROAS WHEN YOU COME— AND THE BOOKS, ESPECIALLY THE PARCHMENTS.
>
> 2 Timothy 4:13

Seven Days Without Prayer Makes One Weak

Of all the duties enjoined by Christianity none is more essential and yet more neglected than prayer.

—Francois Fénelon

The other day I heard a very famous TV personality, who's now in his eighties, say that he never prays. Even more, he never remembers having prayed in the past. Lately several books have been published by various well-known atheists, all proclaiming the nonexistence of God. Clearly, atheists don't pray, and when I think on what they miss, I'm profoundly sad for them. Prayer—talking with and listening to the Creator—is the engine that powers spiritual life. No prayer, no power.

Oh, I suppose those who don't pray—or won't pray—manage to get through life in their own fashion. But I don't think that's the kind of life most of us want to live. I *need* prayer. It sustains me during the rigors of daily life. I'm like the guy whose atheistic friend attributed the answers to prayer to coincidences. The man who was a pray-er said, "Maybe so, but all I know is that the more I pray, the more coincidences happen, so I'm keepin' on with my praying."

I'm with him. How about you?

THE EFFECTIVE, FERVENT PRAYER OF A
RIGHTEOUS MAN AVAILS MUCH.

James 5:16

If I'd Known I Was Going to Live This Long...

Joy and Temperance and Repose
Slam the door on the doctor's nose.

—Henry Wadsworth Longfellow

Even though this quote is attributed to Georgie Jessel, an entertainer from Great-Grandpa's generation, it's always rung true to me. The older I get, the more truth I find in it. When I was young and dancing with Grandma to "The Locomotion" with the volume at full blast, it didn't occur to me that someday it might affect my hearing. With all those fast-food burgers and all the times I turned up my nose at the salad bar—not to mention my desk job where I've sat hour after hour, day after day, year after year with little exercise—is it any wonder I've gained weight since I married Grandma?

Since I've decided that this humorous quote is true, I've also embraced the great corollary that says, "It's never too late to start taking better care of yourself." The human body has an amazing resiliency. Its ability to heal itself is remarkable. I've already started doing whatever small things I can to turn my health around. I've learned to take a short walk on my breaks at work. I've learned how to make astonishingly delicious healthy salads. And although my motions are perhaps a bit more loco than when I was younger, when Little Eva sings "The Locomotion," I turn the volume down, not up.

What do you say to putting down the Snickers bar and picking up a vanilla protein shake instead?

I WILL PRAISE YOU, FOR I AM FEARFULLY AND WONDERFULLY MADE.

Psalm 139:14

The Best Things in Life Are Free

*The bread that you store up belongs to the hungry;
the coat that lies in your chest belongs to the naked;
the gold that you have hidden in the ground
belongs to the poor.*

—Saint Basil

There's a sad story in the New Testament about a rich farmer who focused his time and money on tearing down his barns so he could build bigger ones (Luke 12:16-21). The purpose, of course, was to fill the bigger ones, just as he had the smaller ones. But this man didn't know that his number was just about to be called up. He was going to die. In telling this story, Jesus reminds us of the folly of accumulating riches for this life and being poor toward the things of God.

That farmer needed exactly what we all need—and it wouldn't have cost him anything. He needed… *We* need the free grace of God to anchor our souls. No amount of goods stored in our barns or money stashed in our bank accounts, IRAs, and CDs will anchor us to the only "profit" that matters.

In the Old Testament, we read

about the poor widow who obeyed the prophet Elijah and baked him a small cake with the little flour and oil she had. In so doing, Elijah promised:

"The bin of flour shall not be used up, nor shall the jar of oil run dry, until the day the Lord sends rain on the earth."

So she went away and did according to the word of Elijah; and she and he and her household ate for many days. The bin of flour was not used up, nor did the jar of oil run dry, according to the word of the Lord which He spoke by Elijah (1 Kings 17:14-16).

Her supply was given to her freely because she had obeyed and gave freely. This is counter to the normal way of thinking—that we must scrimp and hoard for ourselves in order to have enough. No, God's way is to give first… then receive.

What do I have that is stored up or awaiting a larger barn? Whatever it is, it must go.

Care to join me for a bit of barn cleaning today?

Treasures of wickedness
profit nothing,
but righteousness delivers
from death.
The Lord will not allow the
righteous soul to famish,
but He casts away the
desire of the wicked.

Proverbs 10:2-3

Many Hands Make Light Work

Opportunity is missed by most people because it is dressed in overalls and looks like work.

—Thomas Edison

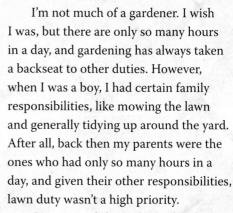

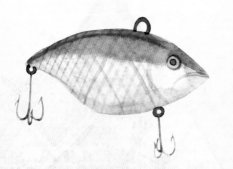

I'm not much of a gardener. I wish I was, but there are only so many hours in a day, and gardening has always taken a backseat to other duties. However, when I was a boy, I had certain family responsibilities, like mowing the lawn and generally tidying up around the yard. After all, back then my parents were the ones who had only so many hours in a day, and given their other responsibilities, lawn duty wasn't a high priority.

Once in a while, we had a family workday where we all pitched in and did something to the yard or house. I'd mow while someone else trimmed the bushes or took a trip to the nursery to buy a new plant. At the end of the afternoon, after we'd swept the porch and washed down the driveway, we were pooped. Even so, we would walk out to the curb, look back at the house and yard, and reward ourselves on a job well done.

Not only did we benefit by working together and accomplishing more, we also enjoyed the day as a time of bonding. Nowadays I suspect families need more bonding time than ever before. Younger families seem to have so many more options that demand their time. It seems that doing things together—like eating a meal around the table at the same time—is rarer than when I was a boy.

It's true that many hands make the work lighter. It's also true that while those many hands work side by side, they are in close proximity to one another. And that's a good thing.

Dirty hands pursuing a common good are better than clean hands folded, doing nothing.

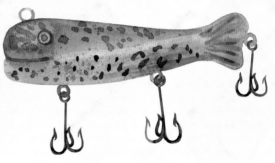

WE THEN, AS WORKERS TOGETHER WITH HIM ALSO PLEAD WITH YOU NOT TO RECEIVE THE GRACE OF GOD IN VAIN.

2 Corinthians 6:1

I Don't Care Where a Person Comes From; I Care Where He's Going

At the heart of racism is the religious assertion that God made a creative mistake when He brought some people into being.

—Friedrich Otto Hertz

One evening after dinner when I was just a boy, my dad brought out an old cruddy-looking box. He opened it and showed me some of the papers that he had kept inside it. They were our family's hand-me-down artifacts—a deed to a long-since-sold property, warranties for century-old farm machinery. One item in particular sent me reeling. It was a receipt for a slave. Apparently one of my ancestors had purchased a slave from one of his neighbors.

I could barely grasp the idea of it. I knew, of course, that my family had deep roots in the South, back to the early nineteenth century. Why then should I be surprised? I guess it was hard for me to come face-to-face with the evidence of familial sins I didn't wish to acknowledge. After all, until that night I could have hoped that *maybe* my family had refused to follow the trend of owning slaves. Were they not Christians? To be honest, I didn't know the answer to that question. I still don't. But now I do know the awful truth that my forebears participated in this nation's worst sin.

Edward Ball, author of *Slaves in the*

Family, had a similar experience. After discovering his family had once owned slaves, he tracked down the descendants of the slaves who had served his family more than a century earlier. I wouldn't know how to do that—or even if I should—but I certainly hope the descendants of the slaves that served my family have fared well.

Most of all, I hope they are my brothers and sisters in Christ and that one day I will meet them in heaven.

We can't do much about the sins of our ancestors, but we can do something to prevent the sins of our descendants. We can instruct them in right and wrong...and even better, we can model it.

For the Scripture says, "Whoever believes on Him will not be put to shame." For there is no distinction between Jew and Greek, for the same Lord over all is rich to all who call upon Him. For "whoever calls on the name of the Lord shall be saved."

Romans 10:11-13

Run with Your Strengths; Shore Up Your Faults

One cannot too soon forget his errors and misdemeanors;
for to dwell upon them is to add to the offense.

—Henry David Thoreau

Have you ever had the foolish notion to write down all your faults? I did. The result was a major case of the blues. The list went on and on. I then decided it might make me feel better to account for my strengths, and so I took out a fresh sheet of paper and began my new list. This, too, was not such a good idea. It didn't take long before I ran out of good points to write down. Why was one list so long and the other so short?

When I finally came to my senses, I realized that though I'm not perfect, I'm certainly not a total doofus. I simply needed to concentrate on the few strengths I listed and not get down in the mouth about the longer list of failings. Better yet, I needed to tear up the list of my faults.

I thought about the apostle Peter in the Bible. Jesus personally rebuked him by saying these harsh words, "Get behind Me, Satan! You are an offense to Me, for you are not mindful of the things of God, but the things of men" (Matthew 16:23). Earlier Peter had seen Jesus walking on water and attempted it himself. He was okay until he became afraid:

So He said, "Come." And when Peter had come down out of the boat, he walked on the water to go to Jesus. But when he saw that the wind was boisterous, he was afraid; and beginning to sink he cried out, saying, "Lord, save me!" And immediately Jesus stretched out His hand and caught him, and said to him, "O you of little faith, why did you doubt?" (Matthew 14:29-31).

In Matthew 26, Peter ends up denying the Lord—despite having assured Jesus only a short time earlier that such an event could never happen. I'm certain that if we made a list of Peter's faults, he might be a tad embarrassed, but Peter was wise enough not to dwell on his failures. He knew that despite his mess ups, he would partake of the glory to be revealed and that a crown of glory was awaiting him (1 Peter 5:1-4).

So along with Peter, let's lay aside our list of faults and turn our eyes instead to the many good things in our lives and the strengths God has given us. A crown of glory! Can you imagine that?

I TAKE PLEASURE IN INFIRMITIES, IN REPROACHES, IN NEEDS, IN PERSECUTIONS, IN DISTRESSES, FOR CHRIST'S SAKE. FOR WHEN I AM WEAK, THEN I AM STRONG.

2 Corinthians 12:10

Freedom Isn't Free

History does not long entrust the care of freedom to the weak or the timid.

—General Dwight D. Eisenhower

Many of us grandpas lost friends in the Vietnam War, the war of our generation. I remember my friends often, Bill and Bruce especially. It seems like every generation has a war to face, a war mostly against enemies who don't like our American freedom.

Freedom is addictive. Once you enjoy it, you don't want to lose it. And so all these years after Vietnam and a century after World War I—dubbed "the war to end all wars"—we still have young men and women paying the price for us to stay free.

My dad was at Pearl Harbor on December 7, 1941, and lost a lot of friends on that infamous day. Before Dad died, I had him make a recording of what he recalled that day. I haven't listened to it yet. I know a day will come when the time will be right and I'll be able to listen to him talk about an event he never spoke much about. Dad wanted to be alone when he recorded it, and I think I want to be alone when I listen to it.

When I see today's young men and women in uniform—usually at an airport—I want to salute them. Some of them will pay the ultimate price just so you and I can remain free.

If you were a warrior for freedom, I salute you too.

THE HORSE IS PREPARED FOR THE DAY OF BATTLE,
BUT DELIVERANCE IS OF THE LORD.

Proverbs 21:31

Happiness Isn't the Goal; It's the Result of Doing the Right Thing

Happiness is like a butterfly which, when pursued, is always beyond our grasp, but, if you will sit down quietly, may alight upon you.

—Nathaniel Hawthorne

For a long time in my youth, I was somewhat of a drifter. I had no specific goals in life—except to be happy. It was later that I learned that happiness is a by-product of making the right choices each day. Somewhere along the way, someone shared with me this simple truth:

Sow a thought and you reap an action;
sow an act and you reap a habit;
sow a habit and you reap a character;
sow a character and you reap a destiny.

—Ralph Waldo Emerson

My destiny, such as it is, probably looks sparse on paper, but to me the happy life I'm enjoying is a blessing. I believe this blessing is a result of two things: making right choices and receiving God's mercy when making wrong choices.

In that respect, making a good life for yourself isn't rocket science. It boils down, really, to a few basic principles, and the most important one is choosing to do the right thing no matter what. Happiness is a by-product of that simple truth. I strongly recommend it.

YOUR EARS SHALL HEAR A WORD BEHIND YOU, SAYING,
"THIS IS THE WAY, WALK IN IT,"
WHENEVER YOU TURN TO THE RIGHT HAND
OR WHENEVER YOU TURN TO THE LEFT.

Isaiah 30:21

All Good Things Must Come to an End

Often when you think you're at the end of something, you're at the beginning of something else.

—Fred Rogers

Like all good things, this book must end—and it does so with a wish for many good blessings to come your way. As you close the cover, turn your thoughts to all the good things in your life. Think beyond your present situation and start looking forward to the future good things God has for you both here on this earth and in eternity.

God's mercies are fresh every morning. We only have to open our eyes and behold them. You have much to look forward to—new adventures, friends you've never met, joys God has yet to reveal.

It's all good.

Really it is.

THROUGH THE LORD'S MERCIES WE ARE NOT CONSUMED,
BECAUSE HIS COMPASSIONS FAIL NOT.
THEY ARE NEW EVERY MORNING;
GREAT IS YOUR FAITHFULNESS.

Lamentations 3:22-23